Temperate Forests

by Sally Wilkins

Consultant:
Francesca Pozzi, Research Associate
Center for International Earth Science Information Network
Columbia University

Bridgestone Books
an imprint of Capstone Press
Mankato, Minnesota

Bridgestone Books are published by Capstone Press
151 Good Counsel Drive, P.O. Box 669, Mankato, Minnesota 56002
http://www.capstone-press.com

Library of Congress Cataloging-in-Publication Data
Wilkins, Sally.
  Temperate forests/by Sally Wilkins.
  p. cm.—(The Bridgestone science library)
  Includes bibliographical references and index.
  ISBN 0-7368-0836-1
  1. Forests and forestry—Juvenile literature. 2. Forests and forestry. I. Title. II. Series.
QH86 .W55 2001
578.73—dc21   00-009916

Summary: Discusses the plants, animals, and climate of a temperate forest ecosystem.

Editorial Credits
Karen L. Daas, editor; Karen Risch, product planning editor; Linda Clavel, designer and
    illustrator; Heidi Schoof, photo researcher

Photo Credits
Erwin & Peggy Bauer/Tom Stack & Associates, 10
James P. Rowan, 6
J. Lotter/Tom Stack & Associates, 12
John Gerlach/Tom Stack & Associates, 14
Ken Layman/Photo Agora, 16
Linda Clavel, 1
Robert McCaw, 20
RubberBall Productions, cover
Unicorn Stock Photos/Marie Mills and David Cummings, 18

Hands On activity contributed by Adele D. Richardson.

1 2 3 4 5 6 06 05 04 03 02 01

Table of Contents

Temperate Forest Facts 5
Temperate Forests 7
Layers of the Temperate Forest 9
Animals of the Temperate Forest 11
Plants of the Temperate Forest 13
The Temperate Forest Ecosystem 15
Monongahela National Forest 17
Temperate Forest Resources 19
Disappearing Temperate Forests 21
Hands On: Sunlight Is Plant Food 22
Words to Know 23
Read More 23
Useful Addresses 24
Internet Sites 24
Index 24

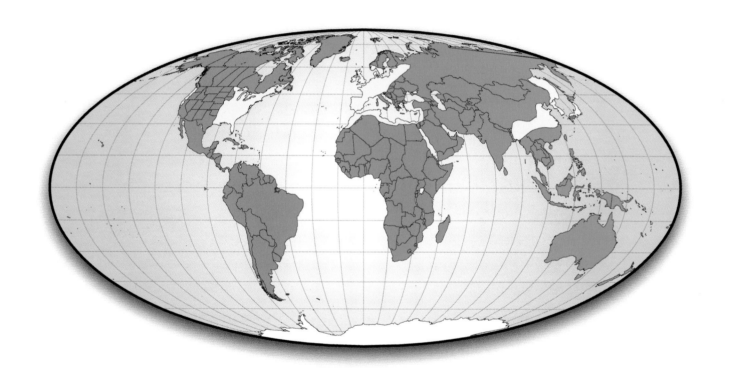

temperate forests

Temperate Forest Facts

- Temperate forests cover about 3.2 million square miles (8.3 million square kilometers) of Earth's surface.
- Temperate forests grow in regions that have warm summers and cold winters.
- Temperate forests usually receive more than 20 inches (51 centimeters) of rain each year.
- Summer temperatures in temperate forests range from 60 to 100 degrees Fahrenheit (16 to 38 degrees Celsius). Winter temperatures fall below 32 degrees Fahrenheit (0 degrees Celsius).
- Temperate forest trees grow a new layer of wood each year. Rings on a log show a tree's age.
- People make furniture and flooring from temperate forest trees. People also make paper products, rubber, and clothing from trees. Fruits and nuts grow on temperate forest trees.

Temperate forests grow in areas where each of the four seasons has different weather. Most temperate forests grow in North America, Europe, and Asia. Summer temperatures are warm and mild on these continents. Winter temperatures usually are below 32 degrees Fahrenheit (0 degrees Celsius). Water freezes at this temperature.

Most trees in temperate forests are deciduous. Oaks and maples are examples of deciduous trees. Their leaves bloom in early spring. The leaves change color when the temperature drops in autumn. The leaves then fall from the trees.

Some temperate forests also have conifers. Pine trees and fir trees are conifers. People call these trees evergreens because they stay green all year. These trees can grow in colder temperatures than deciduous trees can. Conifers have needles. A waxy coat protects the needles from ice and snow in the winter.

Leaves cover the forest floor in autumn.

canopy

understory

shrub layer

herb layer

forest floor

Temperate forests have five layers. The canopy is the top layer of the temperate forest. The tallest trees make up this layer. Many of these trees are the oldest in the temperate forest. The understory is the second layer of the temperate forest. Shorter trees such as dogwoods form the understory.

The other layers are close to the ground. Shrubs such as the mountain laurel form the third layer of the temperate forest. These short bushes grow in shady areas below the understory. Soft-stemmed plants form the herb layer. Mosses and lichens grow on rocks and logs at this layer. Dead leaves and twigs cover the forest floor.

Temperate forests change with the seasons. In spring, the trees in the canopy are bare. Sunlight reaches the forest floor and the herb layer blooms. In summer, trees in the canopy and understory begin to grow leaves. The forest floor becomes shady.

The shrub layer and the herb layer are close to the forest floor.

Animals live at all layers of a temperate forest. Some insects make their homes on leaves in the canopy and in the understory.

Owls and hawks live in the understory. These birds often make their homes in hollow trees. The trees shelter owls and hawks from rain and sun.

Many animals make their homes close to the ground. Mice and chipmunks live in shrubs. Snakes move along the forest floor.

Most temperate forest birds migrate in the winter. They travel to warmer climates. They return to the temperate forest in the spring.

Some large animals in the temperate forest eat plants. Deer and elk walk along the forest floor. They nibble leaves.

Some temperate forest animals such as wolves grow thicker fur to keep them warm during cold months. They shed this thick fur in the spring.

White-tailed deer are common in the temperate forests of North America.

Plants of the Temperate Forest

Most plants in a temperate forest grow at the shrub and herb layers. Their roots grow below the forest floor. Plants take water and nutrients from the soil through their roots.

Wildflowers grow rapidly in the spring before leaves begin to grow on trees. Some wildflowers grow more slowly during the summer when the forest floor is shaded. Other wildflowers die because they do not receive enough sunlight.

Shrubs grow during summer. These plants need little sunlight to grow. Berries grow on many types of shrubs in late summer and early fall. In fall, shrubs receive less sunlight and the temperature drops. They lose their leaves.

Plants soak up much of the rain that falls in temperate forests. They help keep the area from flooding. Their roots keep the soil in place and stop erosion.

Moss grows on trees in temperate forests. Ferns cover areas of the forest floor.

The Temperate Forest Ecosystem

The trees, plants, and animals in the temperate forest are part of an ecosystem. The climate also is part of the ecosystem. Trees, plants, and animals change with different temperatures and seasons.

The trees, plants, and animals in a temperate forest ecosystem depend on each other. Trees and plants provide food for animals. Deer eat leaves and berries. Squirrels store acorns to eat in winter. Insects eat tree bark. Trees also produce the oxygen that animals need to breathe.

Many animals make their homes in trees. Woodpeckers live in tree trunk holes. Other birds build their nests on tree branches. Trees also provide shelter for many animals on the temperate forest floor. Their leaves protect animals from rain.

After animals die, they rot and fertilize the temperate forest soil. They then become food for trees and plants.

Squirrels store acorns in tree trunks. They eat the acorns in winter.

Monongahela National Forest

Monongahela National Forest covers more than 909,000 acres (368,000 hectares) in eastern West Virginia. The Allegheny range of the Appalachian Mountains runs through Monongahela.

Monongahela is a second-generation forest. All of its original trees were cut down. Workers planted new trees when the forest became a national forest in 1920. People now can cut a limited number of trees in Monongahela each year. Workers then plant new trees.

Hardwoods such as cherry, oak, cedar, and maple trees grow in Monongahela. People call these trees hardwoods because their wood is strong. People often use hardwoods to build furniture.

Many animals live in Monongahela. Black bears, bobcats, deer, and coyotes roam the forest floor. Beavers, foxes, wild turkeys, and otters also make their homes in Monongahela. More than 150 types of birds build their nests in the forest.

Blackwater Falls is in the northern area of Monongahela National Forest.

Many of the items people use every day are made from temperate forest resources. People build houses, furniture, musical instruments, and tools from wood.

People sometimes use wood to heat their homes. They burn wood in wood-burning stoves and fireplaces. People sometimes burn wood to stay warm outside. They also cook food over campfires.

Paper comes from temperate forest trees. People turn the trees into wood pulp. They then make paper from the pulp. Newspapers, books, and magazines are printed on paper. People also make paper into brown bags used to carry goods such as groceries.

Some foods and medicines come from trees. Fruits grow on trees. Maple trees produce maple sap. People make the sap into maple syrup. Aspirin comes from willow trees.

People build log homes with lumber cut from temperate forests.

People sometimes cut down too many trees in temperate forests. They waste products that are made from trees. They may not recycle paper products. More trees then have to be cut down to make more products.

People clear forests to make room for farming and to build homes. They cut down trees from an area of a forest. They then burn the area and plant crops. Burning pollutes the air.

Air pollution destroys temperate forests around the world. Pollution from one part of the world can travel long distances. Pollution from factories can create acid rain. Acid rain soaks into soil and kills tree roots. Water cannot travel to leaves once a tree's roots are dead.

Temperate forest animals suffer when their homes are destroyed. They have to move to other areas to find food and shelter. Some animals die when their habitat is cleared.

People clear forests to plant crops and to build homes. They make products such as paper from the wood.

Hands On: Sunlight Is Plant Food

All plants need sunlight for energy. This activity will show you what happens when plants do not get enough sunlight.

What You Need

Piece of aluminum foil
Scissors
Plant with green leaves
Paper clips

What You Do

1. Cut the aluminum foil into small squares. The squares should be about half the size of the leaves on your plant.
2. Clip the squares onto several plant leaves.
3. After four or five days, remove the paper clips and aluminum foil.

The part of the leaf that was covered with foil will be lighter than the rest of the leaf. The spot is lighter because it did not receive enough sunlight. Plants cannot get the energy they need without sunlight.

Words to Know

conifer (KON-uh-fur)—a tree with needles and cones that keeps its needles all year

deciduous tree (di-SIJ-oo-uhss TREE)—a tree that sheds its leaves each year

ecosystem (EE-koh-siss-tuhm)—a community of plants and animals interacting with their environment

erosion (i-ROH-zhuhn)—the wearing away of land by water or wind

habitat (HAB-uh-tat)—the place and conditions in which a plant or animal lives

nutrient (NOO-tree-uhnt)—a substance needed by a living thing to stay healthy

pollution (puh-LOO-shuhn)—harmful materials that damage the environment

Read More

Burnie, David. *Forest.* Inside Guides. New York: DK Publishing, 1998.

Hall, Cally. *Forests.* Closer Look At. Brookfield, Conn.: Copper Beech Books, 1999.

Morris, Neil. *Forests.* The Wonders of Our World. New York: Crabtree Publishing, 1998.

Useful Addresses

Temperate Forest Foundation
14780 SW Osprey Drive
Suite 355
Beaverton, OR 97007

USDA Forest Service
P.O. Box 96090
Washington, DC 20090-6090

Internet Sites

Shades of Green: Earth's Forests
http://library.thinkquest.org/17456/main.html
Smokey Bear's Home Page
http://www.smokeybear.com
What's it Like Where You Live? Forests
http://mbgnet.mobot.org/sets/temp/index.htm
World of Trees
http://www.domtar.com/arbre/english/index.htm

Index

acid rain, 21
birds, 11, 15, 17
canopy, 9, 11
climate, 15
conifers, 7
deciduous trees, 7
deer, 11, 15, 17

floor, 9, 11, 13, 15
herb layer, 9, 13
seasons, 7, 15
shrubs, 9, 13
understory, 9, 11
wildflowers, 13
wood, 17, 19